Cycling in Summer

Cycling in Summer

Joseph Coelho

Illustrated by
Marilyn Esther Chi

Collins

CONTENTS

CHAPTER 1

YAY! I'm whooping and cheering with
Dad as we speed along the bike path by
the canal. I can feel my curls stream out
from my fire-truck red cycle helmet, waving
in the wind.

We've been cycling all morning. The sun is shining, birds are tweeting and as I pedal it feels like I'm flying.

My bike is an amazing machine! I love the way it feels as it glides over the hard mud of the canal path. I enjoy the way it responds to my every move. It's quick – super quick – but also super smooth to ride. I love the way the wind whips past my face. Even though my legs burn when I pedal hard, it's exhilarating, making me feel happy and strong. I don't want the ride to end. I could go on for hours and hours!

But then ...

Disaster strikes.

I don't know what did it. Maybe it was a stone on the path, or a piece of glass. Maybe it happened when I went too fast over a rocky bit we passed earlier. The first thing I notice is that Sheba (that's my bike's name) is not responding like usual. It feels sluggish and slow, and then starts making an alarming noise – an odd squeaking sound. I look down at my front tyre and see that it is flat. Oh no.

flat front tyre

"Dad! My tyre!" I shout. Dad skids to a halt behind me, mopping his brow with the flannel he always has hanging out of his back pocket.

"Your first puncture!" says Dad.

"Do we have to go home now?" I ask. I feel bad that this perfect day might have to end.

"Of course not, July," he says. "We'll have you patched up in no time."

Dad dives into a small bag strapped underneath the saddle of his Torus 1000 bike. (He calls his bike Lion-O because of some ancient cartoon he used to watch when he was a kid.)

He starts getting out all these
specialist tools. Well, really just one tool, but
it's like a puzzle – it has all these other tools
that flip out of it.

"First we need to get the tyre off," says Dad. He takes out this plastic lever thing that actually clips out of the tool, in fact he clips out two of them.

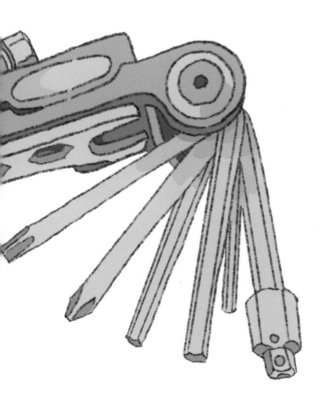

He uses the flat edge to lever the rubber tyre off the metal rim of the wheel.

I watch him curiously. "What are those things?" I ask.

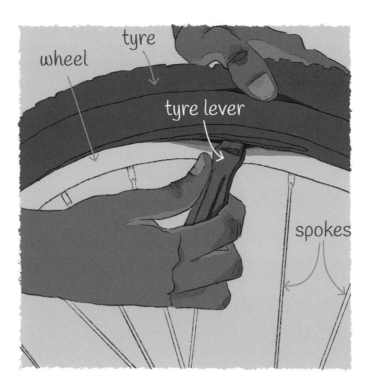

wheel

tyre

tyre lever

spokes

"These are tyre levers," says Dad.
"They're the easiest way of getting your
tyre off." He slides the lever all the way
around the rim, and just like that, the tyre is
half on and half off the wheel rim.

BONUS
ANATOMY OF A BIKE

saddle

saddle stem

carry rack

chain guard

rear light

gears

tensioning cog

stand

chain

handlebars

brake lever

frame

gear lever

handlebar stem

front light

mud guard

forks

disc brakes

pedal

valve cap

spokes

tyre

valve

wheel rim

13

Chapter 2

Inside the tyre I can see this black rubber thing. "That's what we want," says Dad, taking a slurp from my water bottle.

"Hey, drink your own!" I say, because I've got the last of Nan's homemade apple juice in mine and I am making it last.

"Sorry," he grins. He flicks a silver metal lever where the wheel of my bike attaches to the frame. In an instant, he has taken the whole wheel off!

I feel my heart thump. I've never seen Sheba looking so sad. Now the wheel is off, I wonder if Dad will really be able to fix it.

Or am I actually seeing the destruction of my bike?

"Look at this, July," says Dad, as he shows me where the valve is for the inner tube.

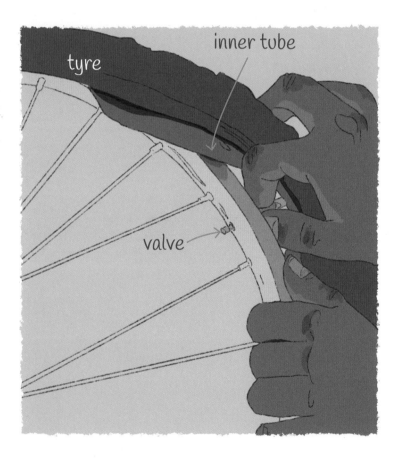

inner tube

tyre

valve

We have to pop the valve through the rim of the wheel to get the inner tube out. It's like a little metal hose sticking out of a hole in the wheel's metal rim. Dad pokes the valve back through the hole. Then he seizes the long black inner tube and pulls it out of the tyre. It's all wiggly and rubbery.

Then Dad does something
seriously unexpected! He takes the inner
tube over to a little puddle by the side
of the path and plunges the tube in to
the water.

"What are you doing that for?" I ask,
thinking Dad is acting strangely.

"I guess it is a little odd, but your inner
tube has a puncture and we need to find it,"
says Dad. "The best way to do that is to look
for bubbles." Dad holds the inner tube under
the muddy puddle water.

"Yuck!" I say, as the muddy water splashes
onto my bright yellow cycling shoes.
There is a little bit of air still in the tube.

Dad starts to squeeze sections of the tube in the water, slowly making his way around the whole tube until…

"BUBBLES!" I shout. I see a stream of bubbles popping up in the puddle.

"Yes!" says Dad. "The bubbles show where the hole is!"

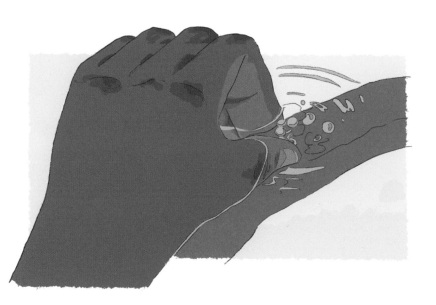

Dad lifts the inner tube out. He's staring at the now dripping section, trying to find where the bubbles were coming from. I'm younger, so my eyes are much better than Dad's. I spot a hole straight away. It's tiny, like a little pin-prick. Without the bubble trick there's no way we would have located it!

"Brilliant!" says Dad. "Pass me the puncture repair kit." I rummage in the little bag under his saddle and pull out a tiny metal box.

"That's it! Open it and hand me the sandpaper," says Dad.

Sandpaper? To my surprise, there is a tiny square of sandpaper in the box, along with a little tube of glue and some black rubber patches. I pass Dad the sandpaper and he starts to rub the area around the hole.

"Hey!" I say. "You're going to make it worse!"

BONUS
PUNCTURE REPAIR KIT

glue

Vulcanizing Rubber Solution

5gms ℮

crayon to mark where
the puncture is

patches to cover
the puncture

sandpaper to rub
on the inner tube

chalk to stop the patch
getting stuck to the inside
of the tyre

CHAPTER 3

"Don't worry, July!" says Dad. "You have to make the area around the hole a little bumpy so the glue can stick! Pass me the glue and a patch."

I'm amazed that all the little things in this box can be used to fix a puncture. Transfixed, I pass Dad the items. He opens the tube of glue and dabs it around the hole, right where he had rubbed the inner tube with the sandpaper. He then carefully places the rubber patch on top and squeezes it down.

It's a bit like doing surgery for a bike.

I picture Dad and me opening up a bike surgery, travelling the country and helping people repair their bikes. I picture us travelling the world: *Webb and Daughter, Brilliant Bike Surgeons for the World* ...

"That's it!" says Dad, breaking me out of my daydream. "All done. All we need to do now is get the inner tube and tyre back on the wheel. Then we can put the wheel back on your bike, and you can get going again. First, though, there's one more routine check to make."

Dad picks up the wheel and starts looking at the interior of the tyre. "We have to check that whatever caused the puncture isn't still stuck in your tyre. Otherwise, you'll get another puncture, and then we'll have to do this all over again."

"Let me look," I say. "My eyes are sharper than yours." I seize the wheel and peer into the tyre, lifting up the edge that Dad had levered off the rim. I go slowly and carefully. The interior of the tyre is lighter than the outside so it's quite easy to see anything that shouldn't be there. I've almost finished checking the whole tyre when I spot it!

I see a little sharp point of something in the tyre. I turn it over and check the outside of the tyre, and there it is: a thorn! A seriously big thorn has gone through my tyre, straight to the inner tube.

What a good job we checked! I carefully
pull it out, whispering sorry to Sheba,
because I know what's it's like to have
a thorn, and it hurts.

"Good job, July," says Dad. "I think you can put the inner tube back now!"

"Really?" I ask. I'm excited, but also a little scared in case I mess it up.

"Don't worry, it's very easy," says Dad. "First, poke the valve through the hole in the wheel's rim and then just push the inner tube into the tyre."

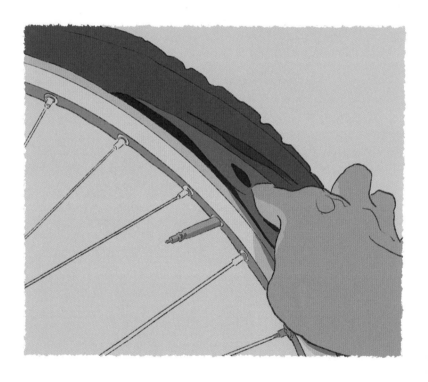

I lift the edge of the tyre and find the hole in the wheel's metal rim. It's a bit tricky getting the valve of the inner tube through the hole, but I do it, and then the rest is quite easy. I poke the rest of the inner tube up into the tyre all around the wheel. But there's a problem!

BONUS
DIFFERENT BIKES

There are lots of different kinds of bikes which are good for different purposes!

This fast road bike can zip through traffic!

On a mountain bike like this you can cycle over rocks and mud.

This bike is called a tandem. Two people ride it at once!

This tricycle has lots of room to carry luggage.

This unicycle is good for doing stunts and tricks!

You lie down to ride this recumbent bike!

35

Chapter 4

The tyre has been levered off, and try as I might, I just can't get it to snap back on to the rim. I get close, getting most of the tyre in place, but there's the last little bit that's too hard to get on.

"I think you're forgetting something," says Dad. I think... of course – the lever tool! I grab it and use my fingers to push most of the tyre back into the rim.

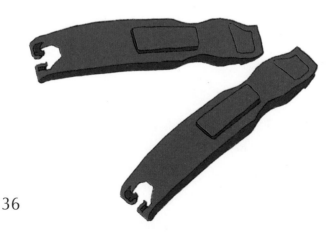

After a while, it starts to get really tight
again, and it's too hard to move the tyre.

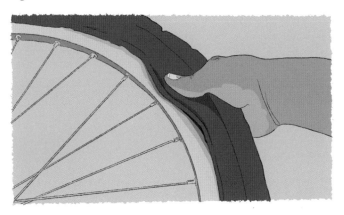

Then I poke the tyre lever under the thick
rubber of the tyre and flip it up. Just like
that, the tyre snaps into place – a perfect fit.

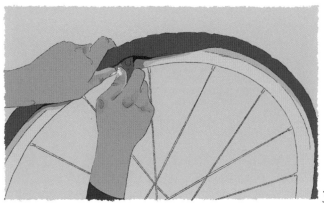

37

Dad helps me line up the axle with the hole on the fork. I'm learning so many new words for the parts of my bike!

axle

fork

The wheel settles into place.

"All you need to do now is click down that metal lever," says Dad. The lever he means is the metal one on the end of the wheel's axle. I click it down and the wheel is locked back into place on the frame.

"Now let's see if it worked," says Dad.
He unclips a bike pump from his bike frame
and starts to pump up my tyre. I have
everything crossed.

Dad gets halfway and then stops.
"Actually, why am I pumping?" he says.
"I guess you should be doing this, July."
And I laugh as I take over.

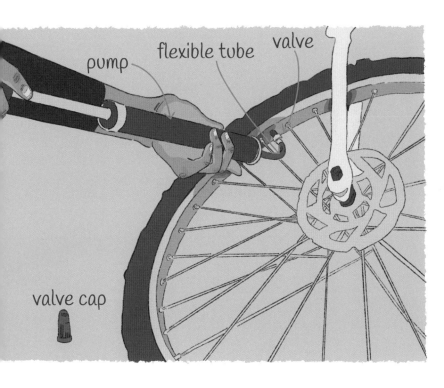

pump

flexible tube

valve

valve cap

It's exhausting work getting Sheba back
to its former glory. It takes a while until
the tyre is rock solid. I unscrew the flexible
tube of the pump from the inner tube valve
and put the valve cap back on.

Dad and I press the tyre all around,
feeling and waiting. What if all our
surgery on Sheba didn't work? After what
feels like hours, the tyre is still solid, and
I feel victorious! We pack up the tools and
jump back on our bikes.

I can't believe I now know how to fix
a puncture! As we start to climb the slow,
winding hills, I daydream – I picture myself
cycling round the world like the world record
holder, Jenny Graham. In my imagination,
I'm cycling across India and getting
a puncture. But it's fine, because I know
what to do, and I picture myself using
the skills Dad has taught me.

Back in reality, we cycle up the hills to the top of the white cliffs. The sea folds out in front of us.

"Fancy a bite to eat?" asks Dad. He has a bag on his handlebars, and inside are all sorts of goodies:

- sandwiches (slightly squished)
- crisps (slightly crunched)
- a tub of grapes (slightly bent)
- some choc chip cookies (slightly melted).

But it's all perfect.

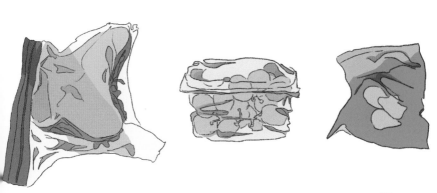

BONUS
REAL WORLD CYCLISTS

Vera Ngosi-Sambrook is an adventure cyclist from Wales. In 2021, Vera was awarded the Ultra Distance Scholarship. She competed in a 2,000 kilometre race from France to northern Wales.

Vera Ngosi-Sambrook

Jenny Graham

Jenny Graham is a record-breaking cyclist
from Scotland. In 2018, Jenny became
the fastest woman to cycle all the way
around the world! This massive trip took just
four months.

CHAPTER 5

The ride home takes longer because
it rains. Not a gentle summer shower
– a proper downpour! But I don't care.
Dad and I yell and whoop as we get soaked.
I'm imagining our bikes are horses and
we're galloping off on an adventure to find
hidden treasure. We get home drenched
but smiling.

The following weekend my friend Carlos calls by with his brand-new mountain bike, saying he wants to explore. I haven't been out that much on my bike without Dad. He takes us to the local park and says, "I'm going to be right here if you need me, but otherwise as long as you stay in the park you can go where you like." It feels like this could be an adventure. Dad checks my bike over and gives me his little saddle bag of bike tools – "Just in case," he says.

47

Topnotch Park is huge. We decide to follow a winding path through it. Carlos is a little shorter than me, but his bike is massive. I wonder if it's too big for him. He's a bit shaky on it at first, but as we get into the ride he gets faster and more daring. Soon he's riding up the grassy banks in the park and shouting as he zooms down the other side. We go further into the park, to a part we haven't been to before. But we're still on the path, so we know we're not going to get lost.

In my imagination, we are two explorers on a jungle exploration in the Amazon rainforest. Then I see a zebra! Not an imaginary zebra, a real zebra! Carlos and I stop in amazement. There is a fence between us and the zebra, and it's walking slowly over a field.

"Look!," says Carlos. He points to a group of zebras making their way up the field. I have to blink and rub my eyes. Am I imagining it? The zebras are walking away from us, but there is no way across the fence. So, we start to pedal furiously, following the path around the fence.

The fence veers off to the right then goes steeply uphill. We have to stand up to pedal hard. I start to climb, and Sheba doesn't let me down. But wait, where's Carlos? He's at the bottom of the hill, off his bike and looking despondent. I turn around and pedal back to meet him. I see the problem – his front tyre is flat.

"Oh no," moans Carlos. "Mum's going to be furious, and I guess I'll have to walk home now."

I smile, because I've been here before, and I know that a puncture is no big deal. "Don't worry," I say. "I've got this."

I seize the saddle bag and pull out the multi-tool. I go through all the steps Dad showed me when I got a puncture.

I take the wheel off and use the multitool to
lever off the tyre.

Next, I push the valve through the hole in the wheel's rim, and fish out the inner tube.

I tell Carlos to check the tyre for anything sharp, while I get to work finding the puncture. The problem is there are no puddles …

SPEED CYCLIST RED WALTERS

Red Walters is a British professional cyclist.
He races for X-Speed United.

Red competed for Grenada in
the Commonwealth Games in 2022.
He was Grenada's first ever track cyclist to
compete in the games.

Chapter 6

How am I going to find the puncture if I can't put the tube in some water? I shake my water bottle, but it is almost empty. I look through the wire fence, and can see the zebras getting smaller and smaller as they head away from us. If I don't fix this soon, we might not reach them.

An idea pops into my head. I remember
the sound that balloons make when
you blow them up and release them, as
the air escapes. I wonder if I can *hear*
the puncture. I take the new pump that
Dad fitted to my bike, and start to pump up
the inner tube.

I pump it rhythmically, trying to get it as full as possible before all the air leaks out of the hole. When the tube is nearly fully inflated, I scoop it up and place it close to my ear. I make my way along the inner tube, listening for the hiss of a puncture. I have to be quick though, before all the air is gone. I think I can hear something...

"I found a stone!" shouts Carlos, holding up a small sharp stone that he has plucked from the tyre.

"Carlos, sssshhh!" I whisper. "I'm trying to find your puncture." But it's too late. The air has all escaped, so I have to get pumping again. This time Carlos stands motionless and silent as I listen.

At last I hear a small hiss. I look at
the inner tube and spot the small cut made
by the stone. I get the sandpaper and
rub, squidge on some glue and stick on
a rubber patch.

Carlos is shocked. "How do you know
all this?" he asks, open-mouthed.

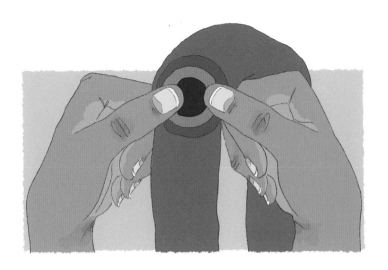

"My Dad showed me," I proudly exclaim.
I replace the inner tube, snap the tyre back
in place with the lever tool and expertly fit
his wheel back onto his bike.

"That was amazing!" he says, as I make him pump up his own tyre. And it stays pumped. I have done it! I have fixed a puncture!

We jump back on our bikes and follow the fence up the steep hill. Our bikes respond to every thrust of our pedals. At the top, we see a sign for Topnotch Safari Park. I had no idea we lived near a safari park, but that explains the zebras.

We watch the zebras as they walk towards the fence, and see a park ranger feeding them handfuls of leaves. There are people inside the park following the pathways. Signs in the park mention other animals like big cats and even rhinos!

I can't wait to cycle back here with Dad and see if we can go inside. But for now, I feel a warm glow of happiness looking in through the fence with my friend Carlos. Not only have I learnt something new, but I've used my new skills to help someone else!

BONUS
BIKES TIMELINE

1825
Draisine

1875
Penny-farthing

1868
Boneshaker

1884
Coventry rotary
tricycle

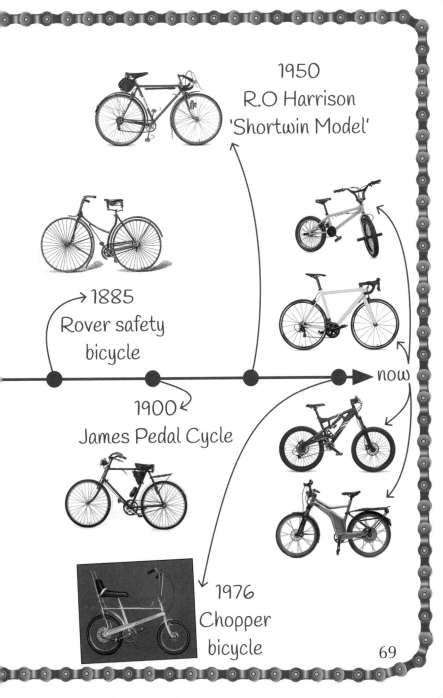

1950
R.O Harrison
'Shortwin Model'

1885
Rover safety
bicycle

1900
James Pedal Cycle

now

1976
Chopper
bicycle

69

About the author

How do you choose what to write about?

I write about things that move me, things that speak to me and inspire me. I have always enjoyed following my interests through my writing, so for instance I get great pleasure from cycling, so these are things I like to write about.

Joseph Coelho

What do you hope readers will get out of the book?

I hope they will enjoy getting to know the characters but also learn a little bit along the way. I hope that my passion for cycling rubs off a little on anyone reading this story.

Is there anything in this book that relates to your own experiences?

I have a safari park quite close to where I live and was shocked when cycling past it one day to see some very exotic animals on the Kentish hills! It was that experience inspired the view of the zebras in *Cycling in Summer*.

What is a book you remember loving reading when you were young?

I would regularly borrow books from the 'oversized' section of the library, borrowing books about UFOs and Mummies and Aliens as well as unexplained mysteries.

I loved finding out about the secrets of the world and hunting for facts.

Why did you want to write this book?

I wanted to share my passion for cycling, but also to let readers know that we never stop learning. There are always opportunities to learn something new, and what we learn can help us in untold ways.

What's the best place you've ever cycled?

I recently cycled between Portsmouth and Plymouth, visiting wonderful towns like Dorchester and riding through tiny villages near the coast. That was quite an experience.

Why do you think it's important to know how to do some bike maintenance?

I think it is hugely empowering to understand not only how something works but also how you can fix that thing should it break. A bike is a very useful, accessible vehicle that can take us on a trip of miles and miles. If you enjoy cycling, like I do, knowing how to fix a bike can mean that your adventures never end.

How old were you when you learnt how to mend a puncture?

I think I was about 11 or 12. I had my first mountain bike and it got the odd puncture so it was much cheaper to learn how to repair it rather than constantly taking it to the bike shop.

About the illustrator

What made you want to be an illustrator?
It was the job that made me the happiest!

Marilyn Esther Chi

What did you like best about illustrating this book?
I thought it was hilarious that I illustrated a book all about bikes, yet I can't ride one. Being part of this let me experience the joys of bike riding in a very different way.

What was the most difficult thing about illustrating this book?
Nothing very difficult, it was just a lot of new kinds of drawings that I don't usually do! I don't often do more detailed illustrations, so there are always nerves with that. But there's so much excitement when creating something you've never done before.

Is there anything in this book that relates to your own experiences?

Not really, I don't ride bikes and I tend to be self taught with most things, and usually learn by getting things completely wrong first! I suppose that keeps me on my toes.

How do you bring a character to life in an illustration?

Expressions! Whether it is facial, a nice outfit, or a fun pose, I think they all help tell the story of a character.

Do you like cycling?

No clue how to ride a bike, but I can definitely fix one now!

Do you know how to fix a puncture?

I do now!

Which of the characters in this book do you most identify with?

Carlos! I like how he just went along with everything. He seems like the kind of friend that makes you braver. I hope I'm that kind of friend.

Book chat

Does the book remind you of any other books you've read? How?

What did you think of the book at the start? Did you change your mind as you read it?

If you could ask the author one question, what would it be?

If you had to give the book a new title, what would you choose?

Which part of the book surprised you most? Why?

Did this book remind you of anything you have experienced in real life?

Who would you recommend this book to? Why?

How do you feel about having a go at mending a puncture, having read this book?

Why do you think July likes cycling so much? Do you feel the same way about it?

Book challenge:
Think of a dream place to go cycling and write a list of what you'd take with you.

Collins
BIG CAT

Published by Collins
An imprint of HarperCollins*Publishers*

The News Building
1 London Bridge Street
London SE1 9GF
UK

Macken House
39/40 Mayor Street Upper
Dublin 1
D01 C9W8
Ireland

ISBN 978-0-00-862461-3

Download the teaching notes and
word cards to accompany this book at:
http://littlewandle.org.uk/signupfluency/

Get the latest Collins Big Cat news at
collins.co.uk/collinsbigcat

Author: Joseph Coelho
Illustrator: Marilyn Esther Chi (Caroline Sheldon
    Literary Agency)
Publisher: Lizzie Catford
Product manager and
    commissioning editor: Caroline Green
Series editor: Charlotte Raby
Development editor: Catherine Baker
Project manager: Emily Hooton
Content editor: Daniela Mora Chavarría
Copyeditor: Sally Byford
Phonics reviewer: Rachel Russ
Proofreader: Gaynor Spry
Cover designer: Sarah Finan
Typesetter: 2Hoots Publishing Services Ltd
Production controller: Katharine Willard

Collins would like to thank the teachers and children at
the following schools who took part in the trialling of
Big Cat for Little Wandle Fluency: Burley And Woodhead
Church of England Primary School; Chesterton Primary
School; Lady Margaret Primary School; Little Sutton
Primary School; Parsloes Primary School.

Printed and bound in the UK by Page Bros Group Ltd

MIX
Paper | Supporting
responsible forestry
FSC™ C007454

Acknowledgements
The publishers gratefully acknowledge the permission
granted to reproduce the copyright material in this
book. Every effort has been made to trace copyright
holders and to obtain their permission for the use of
copyright material. The publishers will gladly receive
any information enabling them to rectify any error or
omission at the first opportunity.

pp12–13 Boris Medvedev/Shutterstock, pp22–23 lee
avison/Alamy, p23 Anton Starikov/Alamy, p34t
stockphoto-graf/Shutterstock, p34b kerozkeroz/
Shutterstock, p35t Vladyslav Starozhylov/Shutterstock,
p35l Peter Versnel/Shutterstock, p35br Ljupco Smokovski/
Shutterstock, p35bl Jeffrey Blackler/Alamy, p44 Courtesy
of Vera Ngosi-Sambrook, p45 dpa picture-alliance/
Alamy, p56 DPPI Media/Alamy, p57 Mark Davidson/
Alamy, p68tl imageBROKER/Alamy, p68tr Lebrecht
Music & Arts/Alamy, p68bl Dorling Kindersley ltd/
Alamy, p68br PA Images/Alamy, p69t Dorling
Kindersley ltd/Alamy, p69tl The Print Collector /Alamy,
p69tr conzorb/Shutterstock, p69cr stockphoto-graf/
Shutterstock, p69cbr silvano audisio/Shutterstock, p69bl
Heritage Image Partnership Ltd/Alamy, p69br Oleksiy
Maksymenko Photography/Alamy, p69b Heritage Image
Partnership Ltd /Alamy.